Sharing Seeds

a donor sperm story for mummy and child

"To my darling wife, the most caring mother,
a heart of gold, often inspirational, always by my side."

ISBN: 978-1-8382256-1-2 (paperback)
978-1-8382256-2-9 (ebook)

Once upon a time there lived a beautiful woman in a cosy house. Every day she would drive from the house to work in her small yellow car, with a smile on her face, but deep down she was a little bit sad.

For the woman, although she had become used to
living on her own, with just her bouncy pet dog
for company, dearly wanted to be a mummy.

To become a mummy, you first need to make a baby.
To do this, you mix a woman's eggs with a man's seeds (also
known as sperm) to create something called an embryo.
This embryo starts off tiny and it grows in the woman's tummy
until it is big enough to come out as a baby.

The beautiful woman knew how to make a baby
but she had no man to mix his seeds with her eggs.

Feeling sad, she visited her wise grandma and chatted about how she could keep waiting for a suitable man to come along.

But the woman did not want to wait any more,
as she knew that she had enough love and strength
in her own heart to be the best mummy now.

Grandma supported her decision not to wait but the next problem was how to make a baby without a man?

So the beautiful woman went to see a trusted
friend who was good at listening.
The woman talked with her friend about
her thoughts and feelings and together
they came up with a marvellous plan -
the woman would go and see a baby-making doctor!

There was a baby-making hospital not far
from the woman's cosy house. Feeling excited,
she drove in her small yellow car to visit the doctor.

The doctor knew of some men called sperm donors.

These men would do kind deeds by donating
some of their seeds so that women could make babies.

And so the doctor mixed some of these special seeds
with the beautiful woman's eggs and created a tiny embryo.

She then put the embryo in the woman's tummy
to grow until it was ready to come out.

After nine months the baby was ready and
the woman became a mummy blessed with her own child.

The beautiful woman is now the best of mummies
to the most wanted child (and a bouncy pet dog)!

The child plays in and around the cosy house with cars
and dolls, dinosaurs and balls and, their favourite toy,
a big green tractor.

Mummy is now radiant with happiness, driving
from the cosy house to work, although she has
had to buy a slightly bigger yellow car!

And together at night mummy and child sit, talk and read books
and, sometimes, a letter written by their sperm donor,
who helped give mummy and her child the precious gift of life.

Beautiful mummy has also become a role model for other ladies who want to start a family, sharing her wisdom and experience so these ladies can go on to become the best of mummies themselves.

About the author:

JR Silver lives in Hertfordshire, England with his beautiful wife,
two blessed donor sperm conceived children and a bouncy pet cockapoo.
JR can be contacted at JRSilver79@hotmail.com or follow him
@JRSilver2 (Twitter) or @sharingseedsbooks (Instagram).
Look out also for more information and future
related book titles at www.sharingseeds.co.uk

CPSIA information can be obtained
at www.ICGtesting.com
Printed in the USA
BVHW021041180122
626500BV00018B/292